P9-CML-440

D0014980

A Note from
Mary Pope Osborne About the

MAGIC TREE HOUSE®

FACT TRACKERS

When I write Magic Tree House® adventures, I love including facts about the times and places Jack and Annie visit. But when readers finish these adventures, I want them to learn even more. So that's why my husband, Will, and my sister, Natalie Pope Boyce, and I write a series of nonfiction books that are companions to the fiction titles in the Magic Tree House® series. We call these books Fact Trackers because we love to track the facts! Whether we're researching dinosaurs, pyramids, Pilgrims, sea monsters, or cobras, we're always amazed at how wondrous and surprising the real world is. We want you to experience the same wonder we do—so get out your pencils and notebooks and hit the trail with us. You can be a Magic Tree House® Fact Tracker, too!

Mary Pope Osborne

Here's what kids, parents, and teachers have to say about the Magic Tree House® Fact Trackers:

"They are so good. I can't wait for the next one. All I can say for now is prepare to be amazed!" —Alexander N.

"I have read every Magic Tree House book there is. The [Fact Trackers] are a thrilling way to get more information about the special events in the story." —John R.

"These are fascinating nonfiction books that enhance the magical time-traveling adventures of Jack and Annie. I love these books, especially *American Revolution*. I was learning so much, and I didn't even know it!" —Tori Beth S.

"[They] are an excellent 'behind-the-scenes' look at what the [Magic Tree House fiction] has started in your imagination! You can't buy one without the other; they are such a complement to one another." —Erika N., mom

"Magic Tree House [Fact Trackers] took my children on a journey from Frog Creek, Pennsylvania, to so many significant historical events! The detailed manuals are a remarkable addition to the classic fiction Magic Tree House books we adore!" —Jenny S., mom

"[They] are very useful tools in my classroom, as they allow for students to be part of the planning process. Together, we find facts in the [Fact Trackers] to extend the learning introduced in the fictional companions. Researching and planning classroom activities, such as our class Olympics based on facts found in *Ancient Greece and the Olympics*, help create a genuine love for learning!" —Paula H., teacher

**Magic Tree House®
Fact Tracker**

HEROES
FOR ALL TIMES

A nonfiction companion to
Magic Tree House® #51:
High Time for Heroes

by Mary Pope Osborne
and Natalie Pope Boyce

illustrated by Sal Murdocca

A STEPPING STONE BOOK™
Random House 🏠 New York

Text copyright © 2014 by Mary Pope Osborne and Natalie Pope Boyce
Illustrations copyright © 2014 by Sal Murdocca
Cover photograph credits: John Muir: © The Granger Collection, New York—
all rights reserved; Harriet Tubman: © North Wind/North Wind Picture
Archives—all rights reserved; Susan B. Anthony: © The Granger Collection,
New York—all rights reserved; Martin Luther King Jr.: © Ronald Grant
Archive/Mary Evans; Florence Nightingale: © North Wind Picture Archives/
Alamy; Gandhi: © Culver Pictures Inc./SuperStock

All rights reserved. Published in the United States by Random House
Children's Books, a division of Random House LLC, a Penguin Random House
Company, New York.

Random House and the colophon are registered trademarks and A Stepping
Stone Book and the colophon are trademarks of Random House LLC.
Magic Tree House is a registered trademark of Mary Pope Osborne;
used under license.

The Magic Tree House Fact Tracker series was formerly known as the Magic
Tree House Research Guide series.

Visit us on the Web!
SteppingStonesBooks.com
MagicTreeHouse.com

Educators and librarians, for a variety of teaching tools, visit us at
RHTeachersLibrarians.com

Library of Congress Cataloging-in-Publication Data
Osborne, Mary Pope.
Heroes for all times / by Mary Pope Osborne and Natalie Pope Boyce ;
illustrated by Sal Murdocca.
p   cm. — (Magic Tree House fact tracker ; 28)
"A nonfiction companion to Magic Tree House #51: High Time for Heroes."
"A STEPPING STONE BOOK."
ISBN 978-0-375-87027-9 (trade) — ISBN 978-0-375-97027-6 (lib. bdg.) —
ISBN 978-0-375-98864-6 (ebook)
1. Heroes—Juvenile literature. 2. Biography—Juvenile literature.
I. Murdocca, Sal, illustrator. II. Title.
CT107.O83 2014   920—dc23   2013012027

Printed in the United States of America
10 9 8 7 6 5 4 3 2 1

Random House Children's Books supports the First Amendment
and celebrates the right to read.

R0440646426

With love for Karin Krause,
who followed a beautiful dream

Historical Consultant:
JENNIFER L. RITTERHOUSE, Associate Professor of History at
George Mason University

Education Consultant:
HEIDI JOHNSON, language acquisition and science education specialist,
Bisbee, Arizona

Special thanks to the Random House team: Heather Palisi; Mallory Loehr;
Paula Sadler; Sal Murdocca for his great art; and Diane Landolf, our editor,
who always makes it better

HEROES
FOR ALL TIMES

Contents

1. Florence Nightingale   13

2. Harriet Tubman   31

3. Susan B. Anthony   47

4. Mahatma Gandhi   61

5. Martin Luther King Jr.   77

6. John Muir   93

Doing More Research   106

Index   114

Dear Readers,

In <u>High Time for Heroes</u>, we met Florence Nightingale on the Nile before she became a nurse. Florence is famous for her work with sick and wounded soldiers during the Crimean War. Later, her work made hospitals better and safer places. Florence devoted her life to saving those who were sick or injured. The more we found out about Florence, the more we wondered how many other heroes did the same thing.

So we tracked the facts! After a lot of research, we chose five other incredible people who made the world a better place. Florence Nightingale, Harriet Tubman, Susan B. Anthony, Gandhi, Martin Luther King Jr.,

and John Muir were each different, but all of them struggled against great odds to follow their dreams.

None of these heroes gave up. When we finished our research, we felt inspired by their courage and dedication. So let's start reading and find out just what makes a hero!

Jack
Annie

1

Florence Nightingale

People have always needed heroes. Heroes inspire us to do great things. Our favorite heroes don't work to have millions of dollars or admiring fans. They believe that there are causes bigger than themselves.

Many heroes have risked hardship, danger, and even death. Their struggles teach us to dream of making a world filled with justice, beauty, and peace instead of violence, hatred, and suffering. True heroes give us hope that if we fight hard enough, this dream just might come true.

A Hero Is Born

Florence Nightingale was born in 1820 to a wealthy family. She and her sister, Parthenope, lived in England in a big house with servants and beautiful gardens.

At this time, girls rarely went to school, so Florence's father taught his daughters at home. Florence grew up to be a tall, graceful young woman. It was rare then for women from wealthy families to work outside the home. Florence's parents expected her only to marry and have children like most other young women.

A Calling

But Florence later said that when she was a teenager, she felt a powerful calling from

14

Florence Nightingale

God to help others. She decided to remain single and become a nurse. Florence's parents were shocked at her choice.

Most nurses then had little training. They were usually poor women who did odd jobs at hospitals. Hospitals weren't like they are today. They were often crowded and dirty.

Many were places where the poor came to die, not to get well. And a hospital certainly wasn't a place for a woman from a rich family!

Elizabeth Blackwell

A Mentor

Elizabeth Blackwell was the first woman to become a doctor in the United States. Elizabeth became friends with Florence while visiting hospitals in England. When the two women took walks together, Elizabeth urged Florence to follow her dream of becoming a nurse. Florence took Elizabeth's advice and began her training in Germany.

17

Afterward she traveled to France to continue her studies. When Florence returned home two years later, she took a job in London as director of a women's hospital.

The Crimean War

In 1854, England, Turkey, and France went to war against Russia. Even though many soldiers died from wounds, many more died from infection and disease. As many as one out of every five soldiers in the Crimean War died, most of them from diseases like malaria, cholera, and typhus rather than battle wounds.

News spread throughout Great Britain that medical care for soldiers in Turkey was very poor. When Florence realized this, she offered to go to Turkey to help nurse the soldiers, but women, even nurses, weren't welcome in military hospitals. Finally, with the

The Crimean War was bitter and bloody.

help of a friend in the government, she got permission to work in an army hospital in Scutari, Turkey. Florence took thirty-eight nurses with her.

Scutari Hospital

When the women got to the hospital, they saw a terrible sight. Hundreds of sick and

Florence's aunt Mai Smith went along to help out.

dying soldiers lay on bare floors or in dirty beds. Most had not washed in months and still wore their bloody uniforms. Insects swarmed over their beds. Because the windows were sealed, the air was so foul it was hard to breathe. Everywhere the nurses looked, they saw suffering.

The windows were sealed because doctors thought that many diseases spread through the air.

There were not enough clean bandages, beds, or pillows. There wasn't even enough food. The men sometimes ate nothing but wormy bread. In fact, there were almost no knives or forks! Florence understood why so many soldiers were dying.

Getting Down to Business

Florence had noticed that patients seemed to heal faster in clean hospitals. She and her nurses began scrubbing everything in sight. Washerwomen fired up great vats of hot water to boil

20

Boiling the bandages, sheets, and blankets killed germs.

bandages, sheets, and blankets. The nurses got busy washing the soldiers and treating their wounds. Florence made sure that each man had fresh bandages and clean sheets instead of ones that had been used again and again.

The nurses also sewed and stuffed hundreds of new mattresses. Then Florence made a chart for each patient, listing what was wrong with him and what his treatment was. Florence was one of the first people to become an expert at keeping perfect records of everything going on in a hospital.

In hospitals today, every patient has a chart listing medications and other information.

Florence even spent her own money to set up a kitchen. A French chef arrived to cook healthy food that would make the men stronger. Within six months, the hospital was in much better shape.

Outrage

When journalists asked her about the hospital, Florence told them about the conditions there. The head of the hospital wasn't pleased. Medicine was a man's world, and he didn't like Florence interfering. As more stories about Scutari came out, however, the English began sending donations for much-needed supplies.

Florence always taught her nurses that fresh air was necessary for good health. Some of the donated money bought windows that opened to let in fresh air and sunshine.

Donations also helped buy the Jeakes Drying Closet Machine, which could dry 1,000 pieces of linen in a short time.

The Lady with the Lamp

Women weren't usually allowed in the hospital at night. There are stories that soldiers often woke up to see Florence carrying a little lantern as she walked through the dark wards, comforting the men. One soldier said that they all thought she was an angel. Florence became known as the Lady with the Lamp.

This picture of Florence as the Lady with the Lamp appeared in the <u>Illustrated London News</u> in 1855.

Florence often visited other hospitals on mules or in broken-down carts. Sometimes she worked twenty hours a day. Much of the time she was sick with what was known as Crimean fever.

Florence was never really well again.

After the War

Florence returned to England as a hero. Although she wasn't well, she continued to work for changes in military hospitals and for the training of nurses. She gave speeches, wrote books, and even went to see Queen Victoria about her concerns.

Even after the Crimean War, people still died more often in military hospitals than in other hospitals.

As a result, the Army Medical College was built to teach military doctors. Florence also founded the Nightingale School of Nursing at St. Thomas's Hospital in London. Florence's ideas about hospitals

Florence sits at the center of a group of nurses who trained at the Nightingale School of Nursing at St. Thomas's Hospital.

Florence was a mentor to Linda Richards, America's first trained nurse.

and the care of patients began to spread around the world.

In 1907, King Edward gave Florence the Order of Merit. She was the first woman ever to receive this honor. Florence died in 1910 at the age of ninety.

During the war, a young soldier wrote a song about her. It says, "One of heaven's best gifts is Miss Nightingale."

Turn the page to read about more heroes who help sick people.

27

Doctors Without Borders

In 1971, some doctors and journalists in France read about a terrible war in Biafra, a state that is now a part of Nigeria. Millions were dying of wounds, disease, and starvation. The doctors agreed that everyone had the right to good medical care. To help people in need, they started Doctors Without Borders.

Doctors Without Borders sends doctors, nurses, and other experts all over the world to help suffering people. They go wherever there's sickness, war, hunger, or a natural disaster. Much of the time they put their own lives in danger. Because they sometimes speak out about the wrongs they see, they've been attacked, kidnapped, and killed.

Today more than 27,000 people from Doctors Without Borders are working in over sixty countries around the world. They work endless hours for very little money. These heroes have saved thousands of lives and have given hope to millions.

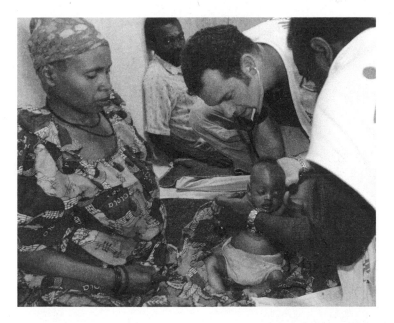

A doctor from Doctors Without Borders treats a sick baby in Bunia, Congo.

2

Harriet Tubman

Harriet Tubman was born in the early 1820s. Because she was a slave, there are no records of her birth. Harriet's parents were slaves on a plantation in Maryland. They named her Araminta Harriet Ross.

Harriet was the fifth child in a large family. After the plantation owner sold three of Harriet's sisters to other plantations, the family lost touch with them. At an early age, Harriet learned that the world she lived in was cruel and unjust.

Early Years

Because slaves weren't allowed to go to school, Harriet couldn't read or write. When she was a little girl, her owner hired her out as a nursemaid to another family. If their baby cried, Harriet was whipped, sometimes several times a day. To protect herself, she wore extra layers of clothes.

When she was a little older, Harriet plowed the fields with oxen and hauled wood. One winter, she worked in a swamp, checking muskrat traps. She got the measles and was so weak that she could hardly walk through the freezing water. Even though Harriet was small, she claimed that all that work made her strong and hardy.

As an adult, Harriet was barely five feet tall.

An overseer watches slaves at work in the fields.

A Terrible Injury

When Harriet was a teenager, an overseer who managed the slaves got angry with one of them. He snatched up a two-pound iron weight and hurled it at the man. Instead, the weight hit Harriet in the head and knocked her out.

Harriet didn't come to for two days. She suffered seizures for the rest of her life. Sometimes she would fall into a deep sleep and couldn't be awakened. Harriet said that since her hair had never been combed, it stuck out "like a bushel basket" and may have saved her from even worse injury.

When she was a young woman, Harriet married a man named John Tubman, but the marriage didn't last.

On the Run

Harriet's owner died in 1849. Harriet thought that the new owner might sell her. She felt it was time to make an important choice. Should she continue to live as a slave, or try to escape to

Harriet Tubman

freedom, even if it meant she could die try-
ing? Harriet chose freedom, no matter what
the cost.

In the fall of 1849, Harriet met people

working with the Underground Railroad. The Underground Railroad wasn't a train that ran underground. It was a secret escape route that helped slaves who were seeking freedom in the North.

The railroad ran north from slave states in the South and went as far as Canada. People called conductors guided the slaves to freedom. Other people helped by offering safe houses where slaves could hide and get food. Some houses had tunnels and secret rooms.

Harriet headed north. She walked at night with the North Star as her guide. Several days later, she crossed into Pennsylvania. Harriet said, "I looked at my hands to see if I was the same person." She said she watched the sun come up like gold through the trees and over the fields. Harriet thought she was in heaven.

Freedom!

Harriet found work in Philadelphia. But she wanted to help other slaves escape. Harriet saved every penny so that she could work for the Underground Railroad. She became an expert conductor. Over the next ten years, Harriet made thirteen trips south to bring slaves to freedom. Among them were her family and friends.

Harriet said, "I was free, and they should be free."

Harriet and her group usually traveled at night in the winter. They walked or rode in wagons. They crossed rivers in boats and slept in safe houses. At times, Harriet wore a disguise to fool people. Once she wore a bonnet and carried two

chickens to look as if she was on an errand. It was dangerous work. Slave owners put up posters offering big rewards for the return of their slaves. If she'd been caught, Harriet could have been sent back into slavery.

Neither Harriet nor anyone she guided

was ever captured. Harriet helped over seventy slaves gain their freedom, and she was the most famous conductor the Underground Railroad ever had.

Harriet the Spy

In 1861, the Civil War began between the North and the South. The South wanted to leave the United States and become a separate country that allowed slavery. Many in the North had come to believe that slavery needed to end. If the North won, there was a good chance that slaves would gain their freedom. Harriet worked for the Northern Army, nursing wounded soldiers. Then the army asked her to be a spy. This was a really scary job. If spies were caught, they would be killed!

Harriet helped Colonel James Montgomery free slaves from rice plantations

Some of the best information the Northern Army got came from slaves.

39

along the Combahee River in South Carolina. With information from other slaves, she found out where Southern soldiers hid along the river. She also learned where floating barrels loaded with gunpowder were.

The colonel's men raided the plantations, freeing over seven hundred slaves.
Gunboats stood by to take them to freedom.
Harriet said the slaves were in such a hurry,
some raced to the boats carrying steaming
pots of rice; others had pigs thrown over
their shoulders!

The Later Years

After the war, Harriet and her second husband, Nelson Davis, lived in Auburn, New

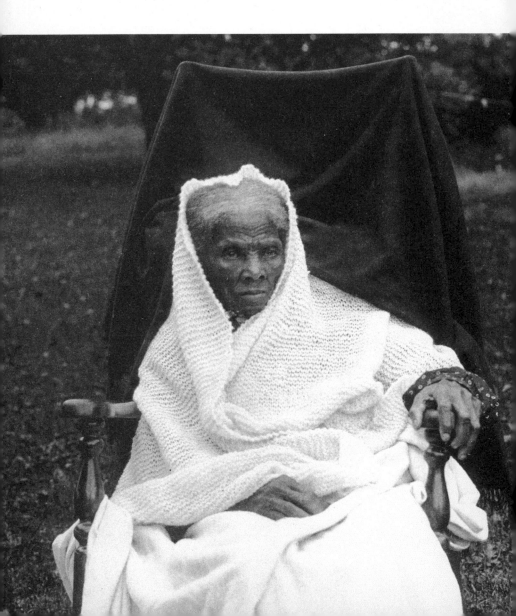

York. She continued to speak out for human rights. Later, she joined her friend Susan B. Anthony to work for voting rights for women.

Before she died, Harriet set up the Harriet Tubman Home for the Aged. She died there in 1913. Because of her work during the Civil War, the army buried Harriet Tubman with full military honors.

Today she is remembered for her amazing courage in helping to end slavery. Many schools are named in her honor, and stores and libraries have shelves filled with books about her life. Harriet Tubman is a true American hero who risked her own freedom to get freedom for others.

"Follow the Drinking Gourd"

Slaves often sang songs called spirituals. Sometimes there were codes in these songs that told the slaves how to escape. One song called "Follow the Drinking Gourd" was especially helpful.

Back then, people sometimes used hollowed-out gourds to drink out of. A group of stars called the Big Dipper is shaped very much like a gourd. The North Star points to the Big Dipper and never changes position. Slaves used the Big Dipper to find the North Star to guide them north.

The song told them other things as well. For example, when they reached a place on the Tombigbee River near the Tennessee River, they remembered a verse that said:

Where the great big river meets
    the little river,
Follow the drinking gourd.
The old man is awaiting for to carry
    you to freedom
If you follow the drinking gourd.

If you were an escaping slave, what
would this tell you to do?

3

Susan B. Anthony

Susan Brownell Anthony was born in 1820 in Adams, Massachusetts. Her father, Daniel, owned a cotton mill. In addition to his seven children, eleven women from the mill boarded with the family. Many people lived together happily in the large Anthony home.

Daniel was a Quaker. Quakers belong to a church called the Friends Church. Like all Quakers, Daniel believed in simple living, education, and hard work. He was also

Susan B. Anthony

Many Quakers were against slavery and worked for the Underground Railroad.

against war and violence. Even though she wasn't a Quaker, his wife, Lucy, shared all of his beliefs. She was a kind and loving mother who worked hard for her family. From both parents, Susan learned to stand up for what was right and to think for herself.

48

Susan Begins

Daniel wanted his daughters to be as well educated as his sons. Susan began to read and write when she was only three.

When she was six, the family moved to Battenville, New York. Susan went to school for a while. But her father thought that girls were not taught enough math, so he started a school at home.

When she got older, Susan became an *abolitionist* (ab-uh-LIH-shun-ist) like her parents. Abolitionists wanted to abolish, or get rid of, slavery. Susan was active in the movement and passed out antislavery petitions.

When her father's business failed, Susan began teaching school to help the family.

The Real Work Begins

Susan taught until Daniel asked her to help him with a farm he'd bought near

49

 Frederick Douglass had escaped slavery. He was a leader in the abolitionist movement and fought hard for equal rights for blacks.

Rochester, New York. Famous abolitionists such as Frederick Douglass often gathered there to talk and make plans. Susan was inspired by their courage.

Women's Rights

Susan believed that women should have the same rights as men. She thought it was wrong that they couldn't vote or hold public office. They also couldn't own property, and few colleges would let them in. There were almost no careers for women outside the home. It was very hard for a woman to earn enough money to support herself or her children.

Women faced many other problems as well. A man could beat his wife, and there was no law to protect her. If her husband took her children away, she was helpless in getting them back. Susan believed that if women could vote, they'd vote to change

51

these unfair things. She began to fight for women's *suffrage*.

Susan and Elizabeth

Susan met Elizabeth Cady Stanton in 1851. Elizabeth also wanted equal rights for women. The two became close friends. They joined forces to fight for women's suffrage. Their friendship lasted for fifty years.

Susan went across the country speaking out for women's suffrage. At times, she cared for Elizabeth's children to give her time for her suffrage work. One year, Susan traveled over 13,000 miles and gave more than 170 speeches. She was always nervous during her talks. Sometimes people shouted or threw rotten eggs at her while she spoke. In spite of this, Susan's motto was "Failure is impossible!" And she really believed that.

Sometimes Susan had to sleep in train stations.

Susan and Elizabeth started a weekly newspaper for women called *The Revolution*. In 1869, they founded the National Woman Suffrage Association to get people to support their cause.

Arrested!

Even though it was against the law, Susan and fifteen other women voted in the 1872 presidential election. They wanted to show how unfair it was that women didn't have the right to vote. The women were arrested and put on trial.

Susan told the judge why the trial was unfair. He gave her a choice between a one-hundred-dollar fine and jail. "I shall never pay a dollar!" Susan said. In fact, she didn't pay *or* go to jail. Susan was not punished. The trial made her famous, and more women joined the cause.

Susan Keeps On

Susan wrote books and kept traveling and organizing. She constantly met with lawmakers asking for a voting rights act for

Susan B. Anthony dollar coin

women. In 1905, Susan even went to President Theodore Roosevelt to ask for his help.

After Susan died in 1906, other women continued the struggle. In 1920, one hundred years after Susan's birth, the Nineteenth Amendment was added to the U.S. Constitution. It gave women the right to vote. Because of Susan and others like her, women all over the country had won a huge victory.

In 1979, the U.S. Treasury Department put Susan B. Anthony's face on its dollar coins to honor her work. Because she'd worked so hard for women's rights, Susan was the first woman to have the honor of appearing on an American coin.

Turn the page to read more about women's rights.

Amelia Bloomer

Amelia Bloomer started the first newspaper just for women in 1849. It was called *The Lily*. Amelia believed in voting rights for women. She also believed in comfortable clothes for women.

It was the style then for well-dressed women to wear tight corsets that made it hard to breathe and move. They also wore long skirts that trailed in the mud and garbage on the streets. Amelia dreamed of soft, clean clothes that let women move freely.

One day, Amelia saw a friend wearing a short skirt with loose, ankle-length pants underneath. Amelia, Elizabeth Cady Stanton, Susan B. Anthony, and some of their friends started wearing this new style. People called their outfits bloomers because Amelia Bloomer had made them famous. A few years later, the women realized that people talked more about their clothes than about their cause, and they went back to their old way of dressing. They would really be surprised by what girls wear today!

4

Mahatma Gandhi

Mahatma Gandhi was born in 1869 in India. His first name was really Mohandas. People later called him Mahatma, which means "great soul." Today most people simply call him Gandhi.

India is a large country with jungles, rivers, swamps, scorching deserts, and the tallest mountain range in the world. There are many different languages and religions. Most people are Hindus, but there are also

Muslims, Christians, Jews, and Buddhists. Each group has its own customs, and sometimes the groups clash with one another.

When Gandhi was born, India was not free. Great Britain controlled it. Since Great Britain was over 4,000 miles away, several thousand British citizens were sent to India to rule over 300 million Indians.

The Gandhi Family

Gandhi was born to a merchant-class family in Porbandar, a city on the southwest coast of India. His father was a leader in the local government. The Gandhis lived in a house with many other relatives.

Fasting means going without food for a period of time.

Every day, Gandhi saw his mother get up early and walk to the Hindu temple to worship. At home, he often saw her praying and fasting.

Boyhood

Gandhi was a shy, skinny boy with big ears. He wasn't very brave. In fact, he was scared of things like ghosts and snakes. Books and schoolwork were his only real friends. For fun, he liked to walk alone in the countryside.

Since Gandhi was also afraid of bullies, he raced to school each morning to get there just before the bell rang. The minute school was over, he dashed back home. Although Gandhi won a few school prizes, he wasn't an outstanding student.

Married!

It was an Indian custom for families to plan early marriages for their children. Gandhi got married when he was just thirteen. His wife, Kasturba, was the same age.

This is still the custom in many places in India.

Gandhi said that he and Kasturba knew nothing about how to be married. They enjoyed their wedding celebration because they could wear new clothes, eat sweets, and play with their relatives. Kasturba thought it was funny that her new husband slept with the light on because he was frightened of the dark!

Gandhi, the Lawyer

Gandhi's family wanted him to become a lawyer. By the time he was nineteen, Gandhi was already the father of a baby son. At his family's urging, he left his wife and child behind to study law in England.

The Gandhis later had three other sons.

After finishing his law degree, Gandhi went back home. Jobs were hard to find. Finally

Gandhi as a young man

65

a law firm hired him to work in South Africa. He was supposed to stay a year. He stayed for twenty-one.

South Africa

At this time, Britain also governed much of South Africa. There were more than 100,000 Indians living there along with the native black South Africans. They worked on farms and in sugarcane fields. Like black South Africans, most Indians were poor and powerless. They couldn't vote and paid an unfair share of taxes.

Because Gandhi was an Indian, a man once refused to sit in the same train car with him. When Gandhi would not move, the conductor threw him off at the next station. Gandhi shivered in the cold waiting room all night. This act changed his life forever. From then on, he vowed to

66

fight for civil rights in South Africa.

Gandhi didn't believe in violence or anger. He felt that love and truth were powerful enough to make great changes. He called this belief *satyagraha* (sah-tyuh-GRAH-hah). Gandhi planned to fight with *satyagraha*, not bullets.

Gandhi led Indians in South Africa in protesting unfair voting laws and other injustices. They were often attacked and beaten. Gandhi spent time in jail. Some people were even killed, but Gandhi and his followers never fought back. When Indians began to get more rights, Gandhi returned home. It was 1915, and he was forty-five years old.

India

Gandhi wanted India to be a free country. To make this happen, he began by asking

Civil rights are freedoms like voting, free speech, and religion that all citizens should have.

A boycott is when people protest by refusing to deal with or buy from people or countries who they think are acting unfairly.

people to *boycott* products made in Great Britain. The government often made Indians buy British goods instead of those that could be made in their own country. It was possible a boycott could hurt British businesses. But Gandhi's main hope for the boycotts was that Indians would feel proud if they could live simply and use only those things that they made themselves.

Gandhi walked from village to village spreading his message of peaceful change. He gave speeches, led protest marches, and fasted for days. Gandhi's fasts came from his strong religious beliefs. The fact that he was willing to damage his health for a greater cause inspired others to join his fight. At times, the fasts made him so weak that he could hardly stand.

As the movement grew, Gandhi organized strikes and urged stores to close to protest unfair taxes. Because he broke the law so often, Gandhi spent a lot of time in jail.

Gandhi went to prison at least ten times.

He asked his followers to be honest, to pray, and to fast. He also urged them to weave their own clothes rather than buy British cloth. His followers called the cloth they wove *khadi*. It became a symbol of freedom.

Gandhi always wore sandals and a

Gandhi weaves cloth at his loom.

simple loincloth that he wove himself. He carried a walking stick and threw a shawl over his shoulders.

Salt March

In 1930, Gandhi planned the biggest march yet to protest a high tax that the British had put on salt. Salt is important for helping the body cool itself down. It was so hot in India that people needed it in their diet to stay healthy. Because of the tax, most Indians couldn't afford it.

Gandhi and seventy-eight men set off to march 240 miles to the sea in Dandi. As they walked, they sang and welcomed other men who joined them along the way. Villagers lined the roads, beating drums and playing cymbals to encourage them. Twenty-four days later, Gandhi led thousands of marchers down to the sea.

Gandhi said a prayer. Then he picked up some salty mud and boiled it down to produce salt. Everyone else did the same thing. A few weeks later, Gandhi was arrested as he slept under a mango tree.

The Salt March sparked protests all over India. Millions marched and boycotted British businesses. Hundreds were beaten or killed. Over 60,000 protesters went to prison that year. Gandhi and his followers

felt that Great Britain's hold on India was getting weaker.

The British Leave India

In 1947, Great Britain was recovering from World War II. It was no longer powerful enough to control India. On August 15, 1947, Great Britain gave India its freedom.

By then, Gandhi was seventy-eight years old. Even though India was free, he continued to work for peace among his fellow Indians. On January 30, 1948, a Hindu who didn't agree with Gandhi's ideas shot and killed him on his way to a prayer meeting.

One Indian leader said that the light had gone out of India. He was wrong. That light still shines today. Gandhi's powerful belief in love and peace still inspires people everywhere. The frightened boy grew up to be one of the bravest men of all.

Kasturba Gandhi

Kasturba Gandhi was a big part of Gandhi's life and work. He often said that Ba, as he called her, taught him much about peace and love. Even though she was from a rich family, Kasturba chose to live a life of poverty with her husband.

Kasturba supported Gandhi's work in both South Africa and India. She was often by his side at marches and walked from village to village with him as he taught people about peaceful protests. Kasturba worked hard to get women to join the movement. She often spoke to them about things like the importance of spinning their own cloth and simple living. She also urged them to join marches and strikes.

Like Gandhi, Kasturba spent a lot of time in prison. Sometimes she even took her husband's place there. Gandhi was at her side when she died in 1944. They'd been together for more than sixty years.

5

Martin Luther King Jr.

Martin Luther King Jr. was born on January 15, 1929, in Atlanta, Georgia. Martin's grandfather and father were Baptist ministers. Martin grew up in a big house full of loving relatives. His mother, Alberta, had been a teacher. When he was five, she taught him to read. Martin's parents raised their three children to treat everyone with kindness.

Segregation means that there are laws that keep people of different races apart from one another.

Separate Worlds

Martin grew up in a time of *segregation* (seh-grih-GAY-shun), when black people didn't have the same rights as whites.

 Even though blacks had the right to vote, states made laws that often stopped them.

This was especially true in the South, where most blacks lived.

It was against the law for black and white children to go to school together. Black people couldn't eat in the same restaurants or sit in the same part of movie theaters as white people. Blacks and whites couldn't even drink out of the same water fountain!

When black people rode buses and trains, they had to sit in the back or stand so whites could have seats.

School Days
Martin was such a good student that he skipped several grades. He entered Morehouse College when he was only fifteen years old. During his college years, Martin began to read the writings of great thinkers,

including Gandhi. Their work inspired him to become a minister like his father and grandfather.

When he was nineteen, Martin went to study in Pennsylvania. While he was there, he continued to read about Gandhi and studied his belief in *satyagraha*. Martin later said Gandhi taught him how to conduct his own fight for civil rights.

Martin continued his studies in Boston and met Coretta Scott, who was also a student. They married in 1953 and later had four children. The couple moved to Montgomery, Alabama, where Martin was offered a job as a minister.

The Struggle Begins

In December 1955, a black woman named Rosa Parks refused to give her seat to a white man on a Montgomery city bus. She

Coretta Scott King was a music student when she met Martin. She was very active in the civil rights movement.

was arrested and fined. When black activists in Montgomery heard about this, they organized a bus boycott, and Martin became its leader. Because most blacks couldn't afford cars, buses were the only way they could easily get around.

But for a year, blacks walked, carpooled, and rode bicycles instead of taking the buses. The boycott caused the city to lose money.

The boycott became big news across the nation. In 1956, the Supreme Court of the United States said it was against the law to segregate buses. The boycott was over, but support for the civil rights movement was spreading, and Martin was ready to lead the way.

The Years Ahead
For the next twelve years, Martin traveled all over the country. He spoke at rallies, in churches, and on the streets.

Martin and his supporters led hundreds of marches and demonstrations. When they were attacked, they linked arms and kept marching shoulder to shoulder. Nothing could stop them.

Martin went to jail about thirty times.

They kept organizing boycotts against businesses that treated blacks unfairly. When they were beaten and spat on, Martin said that only love could drive out hate. Black students and their supporters protested by refusing to leave restaurants and other places that wouldn't serve them. They sat in these places until they were removed by force. These actions were called *sit-ins*.

Volunteers, including many college students, went south to help blacks register to vote. Many were beaten, attacked by police dogs, and sprayed with fire hoses. Some were even killed. Martin and his friends spent time in jail, but they never gave up.

 Martin gives his famous speech.

I Have a Dream

On August 28, 1963, Martin gave one of the most famous speeches in American history. It is called the "I Have a Dream" speech. Over 200,000 people gathered at the Washington Monument for a march to the Lincoln Memorial.

When Martin started speaking, people knew they were hearing something great, something that would never be forgotten. In his speech, he told them that he dreamed of a world where people weren't judged by the color of their skin but by the way they acted. He said he dreamed of a world where black and white children could hold hands together and see each other as brothers and sisters. Martin closed by calling out for justice and freedom.

In 1964, Martin won the Nobel Peace

Prize. The money went to support civil rights causes.

Because of the civil rights movement, Congress passed several important laws. The Civil Rights Act of 1964 made segregation illegal all over the country and also made it against the law to keep someone from getting a job because of their race. The Voting Rights Act of 1965 said that states couldn't make laws that kept black citizens or any other citizens from voting.

Martin's Death

On April 4, 1968, Martin was in Memphis, Tennessee, to march with striking garbage workers. At six that evening, he was standing on his hotel balcony. Suddenly a shot rang out and Martin fell. He died about an hour later. He was only thirty-nine years old.

The man who shot Martin went to prison.

Martin's coffin was carried through the streets of Atlanta on a wagon pulled by mules. Every third Monday in January, the whole country celebrates Martin Luther King Jr.'s birthday as a national holiday.

Turn the page to find out more about Rosa Parks.

Rosa Parks

On December 1, 1955, Rosa Parks took a Montgomery city bus home after working all day as a seamstress. When the bus filled up, the driver ordered her to give her seat to a white man. Rosa, who had been a longtime worker for civil rights, made a brave decision. She knew if she stayed in her seat, she'd be arrested for breaking the law. Rosa refused to move. Her simple protest began a new chapter in the long history of the struggle for equal rights between blacks and whites.

The police took Rosa to jail and fined her fourteen dollars. Rosa kept fighting for civil rights the rest of her life. After she died in 2005, her coffin was brought to the U.S. Capitol so that people could pass by and pay their respects. She was the first woman ever to have this honor. Today Rosa is known as the mother of the civil rights movement.

6

John Muir

John Muir was born in Dunbar, Scotland, in 1838. Dunbar is a cold and rainy town on the coast. John's father believed that everyone, including his children, should work hard. He was a harsh man who often beat John and his sisters and brothers.

John's grandfather taught him how to read and write. They went on long walks together along the ocean. The two spent hours exploring the seashore and its tidal

93

pools. John's love of nature began with his grandfather.

Wisconsin

When John was eleven, his father bought a farm in America and moved the family to Wisconsin. Instead of going to school, the Muir children had to work on the farm. Whenever he could, John explored the nearby woods and fields. He later wrote of his joy at the "young leaves, flowers, animals, the winds and the streams and the sparkling lake."

John often worked seventeen-hour days!

John's father told him that if he wanted free time, he would have to wake up early. John got up at one o'clock every morning! In these early hours, John began inventing things. He created a thermometer so sensitive that the body heat of someone standing five feet away affected it. He invented an "early-rising machine," which was an alarm clock that tipped the bed up and threw the sleeping person to the floor!

He also invented a new kind of sawmill and a horse feeder.

The machine and the drawings for it are lost, but friends of Muir described it like this.

Leaving Home

John went to the University of Wisconsin for two years. He read about nature and began to write down what he learned in notebooks.

John was blind for six weeks.

In 1864, John left for Canada to study plants in the southern provinces. When he ran out of money, he worked in factories. After an accident in a carriage factory, John lost his sight. When it finally returned, he was so grateful he vowed to spend the rest of his life studying the natural world.

Yosemite

John decided to walk a thousand miles from Indiana down to the Florida Gulf Coast. Along the way, he collected plants and slept under the stars. After he reached Cedar Key, Florida, John hopped on a boat bound for Cuba. He returned by way of New York City and then sailed to San Francisco to explore the California wilderness. While he was in San Francisco, he heard about a place called Yosemite (yo-SEH-mih-tee). People told him it had beautiful mountains and valleys and tumbling waterfalls.

John got a job there herding sheep. It gave him time to study the land and marvel at its wonders. He tied his notebook to his waist so he could write down anything interesting that he saw as he hiked. He also spent hours filling his notebook with sketches of rock formations and plants.

John built a cabin and settled in to explore the mountains and valleys. He became especially interested in glaciers and how they helped shape Yosemite.

John began writing articles for magazines and newspapers. He also wrote books. He became well known as a *naturalist*. Famous people visited Yosemite just to spend time with him.

A naturalist is someone who studies nature.

Rancher

After ten years in Yosemite, John married and moved to Martinez, California.

John and his wife, Louisa, grew pears and
grapes on a ranch her father had owned. But

John kept returning to his beloved Yosemite again and again. He'd take along a bag of oatmeal, a loaf of bread, a blanket, and some tea and sugar. "The mountains are calling and I must go," he said.

He also went to Alaska to see its glaciers and the incredible natural world there. John said that no words could describe the beauty he saw.

Over the years, John made many other trips to Alaska.

Saving the Wild Places

John worried that the wild places were slipping away. Logging was causing the great forests to disappear. Much of the land was being destroyed by the overgrazing of cattle and sheep. John wanted to save the wilderness that he loved.

In 1903, President Theodore Roosevelt visited John at Yosemite. For three days, John and the president camped in the wild together. During that time, John hoped to convince him that Yosemite should become a national park.

John's conversations around the campfire with Roosevelt paid off. In 1905, the president made Yosemite a national park. Since then, it has remained an unspoiled wilderness.

John also helped create Sequoia National Park, Grand Canyon National Park, and Mount Rainier National Park. He's known as the father of the national parks.

In 1892, John founded the Sierra Club. Today the club has many thousands of members working hard to protect the environment. When he died in 1914, John had written over 300 articles and twelve books.

Theodore Roosevelt and John Muir stand
on Glacier Point in Yosemite.

103

Our Heroes

John Muir, Florence Nightingale, Harriet Tubman, Susan B. Anthony, Gandhi, and Martin Luther King Jr. are truly heroes for all times. Each of them changed history by following their inner light, by being brave, and by never giving up. That's what heroes do.

Everyone can work to make our planet a fair, safe, and beautiful place to live. Even you can help. You can be kind and caring in school and at home. You and your friends can learn all about the beautiful world you live in. And then you might find a hero in your hearts who's just waiting to be set free.

Doing More Research

There's a lot more you can learn about famous heroes. The fun of research is seeing how many different sources you can explore.

Books

Most libraries and bookstores have books about heroes.

Here are some things to remember when you're using books for research:

1. You don't have to read the whole book. Check the table of contents and the index to find the topics you're interested in.

2. Write down the name of the book.

When you take notes, make sure you write down the name of the book in your notebook so you can find it again.

3. Never copy exactly from a book.

When you learn something new from a book, put it in your own words.

4. Make sure the book is <u>nonfiction</u>.

Some books tell make-believe stories about heroes. Make-believe stories are called *fiction*. They're fun to read, but not good for research.

Research books have facts and tell true stories. They are called *nonfiction*. A librarian or teacher can help you make sure the books you use for research are nonfiction.

Here are some good nonfiction books about our heroes:

- *The Camping Trip That Changed America* by Barb Rosenstock
- *Florence Nightingale* by Shannon Zemlicka
- *Gandhi* by Amy Pastan
- *Harriet Tubman: A Woman of Courage* by the editors of *TIME for Kids* with Renée Skelton
- *Martin's Big Words: The Life of Dr. Martin Luther King, Jr.,* by Doreen Rappaport
- *Susan B. Anthony: Fighter for Women's Rights* by Deborah Hopkinson

Museums, Parks, and Landmarks

Many museums and parks and historic landmarks have exhibits about our favorite heroes. These places can help you learn more about our heroes.

When you go to a museum, park, or historic landmark:

1. Be sure to take your notebook!
Write down anything that catches your interest. Draw pictures, too!

2. Ask questions.
There are almost always people at museums, parks, and historic landmarks who can help you find what you're looking for.

3. Check the calendar.

Many museums, parks, and historic landmarks have special events and activities just for kids!

Here are some museums, parks, and historic landmarks that have exhibits about our heroes:

- American Museum of Nursing, Arizona State University (Tempe)
- Dayton International Peace Museum (Ohio)
- Harriet Tubman Museum and Educational Center (Cambridge, Maryland)
- John Muir National Historic Site (Martinez, California)
- Martin Luther King Jr. National Historic Site (Atlanta)
- National Susan B. Anthony Museum and House (Rochester, New York)
- Yosemite National Park (California)

DVDs

There are some great nonfiction DVDs about our heroes. As with books, make sure the DVDs you watch for research are nonfiction!

Check your library or video store for these and other nonfiction titles about our heroes:

- *John Muir in the New World* from PBS
- *Our Friend, Martin* from 20th Century Fox Home Entertainment
- *Underground Railroad* from The History Channel

The Internet

Many websites have lots of facts about famous heroes. Some also have games and activities that can help make learning about our heroes even more fun.

Ask your teacher or your parents to help you find more websites like these:

- bbc.co.uk/schools/primaryhistory /famouspeople/florence_nightingale
- ducksters.com/biography/women _leaders/harriet_tubman.php
- enchantedlearning.com/history/asia /india/gandhi
- enchantedlearning.com/history/us/MLK
- kids.nationalgeographic.com/kids/stories /peopleplaces/harriettubman
- www.nps.gov/jomu/index.htm

Good luck!

Index

abolitionists, 49–51
Adams,
  Massachusetts, 47
Alaska, 101
Anthony, Daniel,
  47–49
Anthony, Lucy Read,
  48
Anthony, Susan B.,
  43, 47–57, 58, 104
  arrest of, 55
  coin honoring, 56,
    57
  death of, 56
  education and,
    47–49
  family of, 47–49
Army Medical
  College, 25
Atlanta, Georgia,
  77, 89

Auburn, New York,
  42–43

Battenville, New
  York, 49
Biafra, 28
Big Dipper, 44
Blackwell,
  Elizabeth, 17
Bloomer, Amelia,
  58–59
Boston, 80
boycotts, 68, 72,
  80–82, 84
Bunia, Congo, 29

Canada, 36, 96
Cedar Key, Florida,
  98
cholera, 18
civil rights, 43, 50,

66–67, 78–79, 80–91; *see also* voting rights

Civil Rights Act of 1964, 88

Civil War, 39–41, 42, 43

clothing, 58–59, 69–70

Combahee River, 40

Crimean War, 18–25, 27

Cuba, 98

Dandi, India, 70

Davis, Nelson, 42

diseases, 18, 20, 25, 28, 32

doctors, 16, 17, 20, 25, 28–29

Doctors Without Borders, 28–29

Douglass,

Frederick, 50

Dunbar, Scotland, 93

Edward, King, 26

England, s*ee* Great Britain

fasting, 62, 68, 69

Florida, 96–98

"Follow the Drinking Gourd," 44–45

France, 18, 22, 28

freedom, 34–41, 43, 62, 67, 69, 73, 87

Friends Church, *see* Quakers

Gandhi, Kasturba, 64–65, 74–75

Gandhi, Mahatma, 61–75, 80, 104

childhood, 62–65

death of, 73
education of,
  63–64, 65
family of, 62, 65
health of, 68
imprisonment of,
  67, 69, 72, 75
marriage of,
  64–65, 74–75
protests by, 66–73
Germany, 17
germs, 16, 21
Glacier Point, 103
Grand Canyon
  National Park,
  102
Great Britain, 14,
  17, 18, 23, 25, 62,
  65, 66, 68–73

Harriet Tubman
  Home for the
  Aged, 43

heroes, 13–14, 25,
  29, 43, 104
Hinduism, 61–62, 73
hospitals, 15–26
  charts in, 22

"I Have a Dream"
  speech, 86, 87
*Illustrated London
  News*, 24
India, 61–73, 74
Indiana, 96

Jeakes Drying
  Closet Machine,
  23

khadi, 69
King, Alberta, 77
King, Coretta Scott,
  80, 81
King, Martin Luther,
  Jr., 77–89, 104

birthday of, 77, 89
death of, 88–89
education of, 77,
79–80
imprisonment of, 84
marriage of, 80, 81
speeches given by,
86, 87

Lady with the Lamp,
24; *see also*
Nightingale,
Florence
Lily, The, 58
Lincoln Memorial,
87
London, England,
18, 25

malaria, 18
marches, 68, 70–73,
74, 83, 87, 88
Martinez,

California, 99
Maryland, 31
measles, 32
Memphis,
Tennessee, 88
Montgomery,
Alabama, 80
bus boycott in,
80–82, 90–91
Montgomery, James,
39, 41
Morehouse College,
79
Mount Rainier
National Park,
102
Muir, John, 93–103,
104
education of, 93–94,
96
inventions of, 94–95
marriage of, 99–100
Muir, Louisa, 100

national parks, 102
National Woman
   Suffrage
   Association, 54
naturalists, 99
newspapers, 54, 58, 99
New York, 42–43,
   49, 50, 98
New York City, 98
Nigeria, 28
Nightingale,
   Florence, 13–27,
   104
   education and
   training of, 14,
   17–18
   family of, 14–15
   health of, 25
   innovations of,
   20–22
Nightingale,
   Parthenope, 14
Nightingale School

   of Nursing, 25,
   26
Nineteenth
   Amendment, 56
Nobel Peace Prize,
   87–88
Northern Army, 39
North Star, 36, 44
nurses, 15–27, 28, 39

Order of Merit, 26

Parks, Rosa, 80–82,
   89, 90–91
Pasteur, Louis, 16
Pennsylvania, 36,
   37, 80
Philadelphia, 37
Porbandar, India, 62

Quakers, 47–48

religion, 61–62, 67,

68, 69, 72, 73, 77, 80

Revolution, The, 54

Richards, Linda, 26

Rochester, New York, 50

Roosevelt, Theodore, 56, 101–103

Russia, 18

Salt March, 70–73

San Francisco, 98

satyagraha, 67, 80

Scutari Hospital, 19–25

segregation, 78–79, 82, 88

Sequoia National Park, 102

Sierra Club, 102

sit-ins, 84

slavery, 31–43,

44–45, 48, 49–51

Smith, Mai, 19

soldiers, 18–25, 27, 39, 40

South Africa, 66–67, 74

South Carolina, 40

spirituals, 44–45

St. Thomas's Hospital, 25, 26

Stanton, Elizabeth Cady, 53–54, 58

strikes, 68, 74, 88

suffrage, *see* voting rights

Supreme Court of the United States, 82

taxes, 66, 69, 70

Tennessee River, 44

Tombigbee River, 44

Tubman, Harriet,

31–43, 104
death of, 43
family of, 31–32
health of, 32, 34
marriages of, 34, 42
spying by, 39–41, 43
Tubman, John, 34
Turkey, 18, 19
typhus, 18

Underground
  Railroad, 36–39,
  48; *see also*
  slavery
University of
  Wisconsin, 96
U.S. Capitol, 91
U.S. Congress, 88
U.S. Constitution,
  56
U.S. Treasury
  Department, 57

Victoria, Queen, 25
voting rights, 43,
  51–56, 58–59,
  66–67, 78, 84, 88;
  see also civil
  rights; women's
  rights
Voting Rights Act
  of 1965, 88

Washington
  Monument, 87
Wisconsin, 94, 96
women's rights, 15,
  18, 22–23, 43,
  51–59, 74, 91
World War II, 73

Yosemite, 96–103

Photographs courtesy of:

© Culver Pictures Inc./SuperStock (front cover: Gandhi). © Dinodia Photos/Alamy (p. 75). © DIZ München GmbH, Süddeutsche Zeitung Photo/Alamy (pp. 65, 69). © Epic/Mary Evans Picture Library (p. 81). © Everett Collection Inc./Alamy (p. 48). © Maurizio_Gambarini/picture-alliance/dpa/AP Images (p. 29). © The Granger Collection, New York—all rights reserved (front cover: John Muir, Susan B. Anthony, pp. 17, 35, 38, 42, 50, 100, 103). © Illustrated London News Ltd./Mary Evans (p. 23). © INTERFOTO/Alamy (p. 15). © INTERFOTO/Sammlung Rauch/Mary Evans (pp. 24, 33). © Richard Levine/Alamy (p. 56). © Look and Learn/The Bridgeman Art Library (p. 19). © National Geographic Stock: Vintage Collection/The Granger Collection, New York—all rights reserved (p. 97). © North Wind Picture Archives/Alamy (front cover: Florence Nightingale). © North Wind/North Wind Picture Archives—all rights reserved (front cover: Harriet Tubman). © Ronald Grant Archive/Mary Evans (front cover: Martin Luther King Jr.). © Rue des Archives/The Granger Collection, New York—all rights reserved (pp. 83, 86). © ullstein bild/The Granger Collection, New York—all rights reserved (p. 72). © Wellcome Library, London (p. 26). © Jim West/Alamy (p. 105).

Have you read the adventure that
matches up with this book?

Don't miss Magic Tree House® #51

High Time for Heroes

When the magic tree house whisks them
to Egypt, Jack and Annie meet one of
the most famous and beloved nurses in
history—Florence Nightingale! But
Florence isn't sure she has what it
takes to be a great hero. Can Jack
and Annie help her find her way?

If you're looking forward to
Magic Tree House® #52: *Soccer on Sunday,*
you'll love finding out the facts
behind the fiction in

Magic Tree House®
Fact Tracker

SOCCER

A nonfiction companion to
Magic Tree House® #52:
Soccer on Sunday

It's Jack and Annie's very own guide
to soccer.

Coming in May 2014!

Have you ever wanted to keep your own
special notebook, just like Jack?

Coming in April 2014!

Adventure awaits at

MagicTreeHouse.com

You've Read the Books ... Now Play the Games!

Join Jack and Annie on brand-new missions and play the Fact Tracker Showdown!

Exclusive to You!
Use this code
to unlock a sneak peek at
MAGIC TREE HOUSE #51:
HIGH TIME FOR HEROES

REWARD CODE

EGYPT

© 2011 Mary Pope Osborne. Magic Tree House is a registered trademark of Mary Pope Osborne; used under license.

MAGIC TREE HOUSE®

MTHFT28

RHCB

Magic Tree House® Books

#1: Dinosaurs Before Dark

#2: The Knight at Dawn

#3: Mummies in the Morning

#4: Pirates Past Noon

#5: Night of the Ninjas

#6: Afternoon on the Amazon

#7: Sunset of the Sabertooth

#8: Midnight on the Moon

#9: Dolphins at Daybreak

#10: Ghost Town at Sundown

#11: Lions at Lunchtime

#12: Polar Bears Past Bedtime

#13: Vacation Under the Volcano

#14: Day of the Dragon King

#15: Viking Ships at Sunrise

#16: Hour of the Olympics

#17: Tonight on the *Titanic*

#18: Buffalo Before Breakfast

#19: Tigers at Twilight

#20: Dingoes at Dinnertime

#21: Civil War on Sunday

#22: Revolutionary War on Wednesday

#23: Twister on Tuesday

#24: Earthquake in the Early Morning

#25: Stage Fright on a Summer Night

#26: Good Morning, Gorillas

#27: Thanksgiving on Thursday

#28: High Tide in Hawaii

Merlin Missions

#29: Christmas in Camelot

#30: Haunted Castle on Hallows Eve

#31: Summer of the Sea Serpent

#32: Winter of the Ice Wizard

#33: Carnival at Candlelight

#34: Season of the Sandstorms

#35: Night of the New Magicians

#36: Blizzard of the Blue Moon

#37: Dragon of the Red Dawn

#38: Monday with a Mad Genius

#39: Dark Day in the Deep Sea

#40: Eve of the Emperor Penguin

#41: Moonlight on the Magic Flute

#42: A Good Night for Ghosts

#43: Leprechaun in Late Winter

#44: A Ghost Tale for Christmas Time

#45: A Crazy Day with Cobras

#46: Dogs in the Dead of Night

#47: Abe Lincoln at Last!

#48: A Perfect Time for Pandas

#49: Stallion by Starlight

#50: Hurry Up, Houdini!

#51: High Time for Heroes

Magic Tree House® Fact Trackers

DINOSAURS
KNIGHTS AND CASTLES
MUMMIES AND PYRAMIDS
PIRATES
RAIN FORESTS
SPACE
TITANIC
TWISTERS AND OTHER TERRIBLE STORMS
DOLPHINS AND SHARKS
ANCIENT GREECE AND THE OLYMPICS
AMERICAN REVOLUTION
SABERTOOTHS AND THE ICE AGE
PILGRIMS
ANCIENT ROME AND POMPEII
TSUNAMIS AND OTHER NATURAL DISASTERS
POLAR BEARS AND THE ARCTIC
SEA MONSTERS
PENGUINS AND ANTARCTICA
LEONARDO DA VINCI
GHOSTS
LEPRECHAUNS AND IRISH FOLKLORE
RAGS AND RICHES: KIDS IN THE TIME OF CHARLES DICKENS
SNAKES AND OTHER REPTILES
DOG HEROES
ABRAHAM LINCOLN
PANDAS AND OTHER ENDANGERED SPECIES
HORSE HEROES
HEROES FOR ALL TIMES

More Magic Tree House®

GAMES AND PUZZLES FROM THE TREE HOUSE
MAGIC TRICKS FROM THE TREE HOUSE

MAGIC TREE HOUSE®

Jack & Annie On Stage

For Live Event Information:
MagicTreeHouseOnStage.com

Now available!
Magic Tree House: *The Musical CD*

760